Pebble™ Plus

Dinosaurs and Prehistoric Animals

Triceratops

by Helen Frost

Consulting Editor: Gail Saunders-Smith, PhD

Consultant: Jack Horner
Curator of Paleontology
Museum of the Rockies
Bozeman, Montana

Capstone
press

Mankato, Minnesota

Pebble Plus is published by Capstone Press,
151 Good Counsel Drive, P.O. Box 669, Mankato, Minnesota 56002.
www.capstonepress.com

1 2 3 4 5 6 10 09 08 07 06 05

Library of Congress Cataloging-in-Publication Data
Frost, Helen, 1949–
    Triceratops / by Helen Frost.
    p. cm.—(Pebble plus—dinosaurs and prehistoric animals)
    Includes bibliographical references and index.
    ISBN 0-7368-3650-0 (hardcover)
    ISBN 0-7368-5107-0 (paperback)
    1. Triceratops—Juvenile literature. I. Title. II. Series.
QE862.O65F78 2005
567.915'8—dc22   2004011094

Summary: Simple text and illustrations present triceratops, its body parts, and behavior.

Editorial Credits
Martha E. H. Rustad, editor; Linda Clavel, designer; Jon Hughes, illustrator; Wanda Winch, photo researcher;
    Scott Thoms, photo editor

Photo Credit
Unicorn Stock Photos/A. Gurmankin, 21

The author thanks the children's library staff at the Allen County Public Library in Fort Wayne, Indiana,
for research assistance.

Note to Parents and Teachers

The Dinosaurs and Prehistoric Animals set supports national science standards related to
the evolution of life. This book describes and illustrates triceratops. The images support
early readers in understanding the text. The repetition of words and phrases helps early
readers learn new words. This book also introduces early readers to subject-specific
vocabulary words, which are defined in the Glossary section. Early readers may need
assistance to read some words and to use the Table of Contents, Glossary, Read More,
Internet Sites, and Index sections of the book.

Table of Contents

A Three-Horned Dinosaur

Triceratops was a dinosaur
with three horns on its face.
Triceratops had a heavy body
and a big head.

Triceratops lived
in prehistoric times.
It lived about 70 million
years ago on plains
in North America.

How Triceratops Looked

Triceratops was about
as long as a school bus.
It was about 30 feet
(9 meters) long.

Triceratops had

two long horns

above its eyes.

It had one short horn

on its nose.

A large frill fanned out

around the neck

of triceratops.

Triceratops had

four strong legs.

It walked

across the plains.

What Triceratops Did

Triceratops traveled
in herds. Herds moved
from place to place
looking for food.

Triceratops cut plants
with its strong beak.
Triceratops chewed plants
with rows of flat teeth.

The End of Triceratops

Triceratops died out about
65 million years ago.
No one knows why they
all died. You can see
triceratops fossils in museums.

Horned Dinosaurs

Glossary

dinosaur—a large reptile that lived on land in prehistoric times

fossil—the remains or traces of an animal or a plant, preserved as rock

frill—a bony collar that fans out around an animal's neck

herd—a large group of animals

horn—a hard, bony growth on the heads of some animals

museum—a place where interesting objects of art, history, or science are shown

North America—the continent in the Western Hemisphere that includes the United States, Canada, Mexico, and Central America

prehistoric—very, very old; prehistoric means belonging to a time before history was written down.

Read More

Cohen, Daniel. *Triceratops.* Discovering Dinosaurs. Mankato, Minn.: Bridgestone Books, 2001.

Dahl, Michael. *Three-horn: The Adventure of Triceratops.* Dinosaur World. Minneapolis: Picture Window Books, 2004.

Gray, Susan H. *Triceratops.* Exploring Dinosaurs. Chanhassen, Minn.: Child's World, 2004.

Schomp, Virginia. *Triceratops and Other Horned Plant-Eaters.* Prehistoric World. New York: Benchmark Books, 2003.

Internet Sites

FactHound offers a safe, fun way to find Internet sites related to this book. All of the sites on FactHound have been researched by our staff.

Here's how:

1. Visit *www.facthound.com*

2. Type in this special code **0736836500** for age-appropriate sites. Or enter a search word related to this book for a more general search.

3. Click on the **Fetch It** button.

FactHound will fetch the best sites for you!

Index

Word Count: 139
Grade Level: 1
Early-Intervention Level: 14